D1156966

THE LITTLE
BOOK
ABOUT
THE
BIBLE

ron rhodes

HARVEST HOUSE PUBLISHERS
EUGENE, OREGON

Cover by Dugan Design Group, Bloomington, Minnesota

THE LITTLE BOOK ABOUT THE BIBLE
Copyright © 2013 by Ron Rhodes
Published by Harvest House Publishers
Eugene, Oregon 97402
www.harvesthousepublishers.com

ISBN 978-0-7369-5181-4 (hardcover)
ISBN 978-0-7369-5182-1 (eBook)

Printed in China

13 14 15 16 17 18 19 20 21 / FC-CD / 10 9 8 7 6 5 4 3 2 1

Contents

INTRODUCTION

Thank you for your interest in this book! I pray that even though it is a little book, it will bring a big blessing to your life. It is uniquely formatted...

▶ Each chapter is short—just two pages.

▶ Each chapter begins by stating the big idea.

▶ This is followed by bullet points that concisely expand on the big idea, with Bible references where appropriate.

▶ Many chapters include other lists that provide key insights related to the big idea.

▶ I then summarize the most important points so you can remember and reflect on them.

▶ Each chapter closes with a thoughtful quote from a recent or not-so-recent Christian leader.

This abbreviated format allows for maximum information in minimal space. This is a little book, but it contains lots of information. Feel free to look up some of the verses I cite. That will greatly enrich your study.

Here's an added benefit of the book. Because it contains 28 chapters, it is ideally suited for four weeks of brief daily devotions on the doctrine of the Bible.

The Silver Cover

The color of the cover of this little book is significant. Silver has long represented truth, revelation, and Scripture. As Psalm 12:6 puts it, "The words of the LORD are pure words, like silver refined in a furnace on the ground, purified seven times."

Illumination Through Prayer

There is great wisdom in beginning each chapter with a short prayer. Ask God to open your spiritual eyes so that you can fully grasp what He wants you to understand (Psalm 119:18). As you study, remember that the Bible is like...

▶ A manufacturer's handbook—it instructs us how to operate our lives.

▶ A pair of glasses—it helps us to see spiritual realities clearly.

▶ A lamp—it sheds light on our path (Psalm 119:105).

▶ An anchor—it prevents us from being swept away by adversity.

▶ A solid meal—it provides spiritual nourishment for our souls.

▶ A love letter—it reveals God's great love for us.

1

An Overview of the Bible

THE BIG IDEA

The Bible is a big book comprised of 66 smaller books, all united by a common theme of redemption.

What You Need to Know

- ▶ The word "Bible" comes from the Greek word *biblos,* which means "book."

- ▶ The Bible is not a single volume, but an entire library of 66 books. It includes letters (epistles), histories, Gospels, poems, prayers, and other kinds of literature.

- ▶ These writings were penned by many authors who lived in various lands and circumstances.

- ▶ From Genesis to Revelation, the Bible tells one primary story of redemption. This story runs like a thread through the entire Bible. Though the story includes many different people, we read of God's redeeming work in each book of the Bible.

Points to Remember

1. The Bible is God's book of redemption.
2. The Father came up with the plan of redemption (Romans 8:29-30; Ephesians 1:4).
3. Jesus then came into the world as the Savior and Redeemer (Matthew 1:21; John 3:17).
4. The Holy Spirit gives believers new life at the moment of conversion (Titus 3:5) and seals them for redemption (Ephesians 4:30).
5. Rejoice that you are among the redeemed!

A Quote to Ponder

"I never knew all there was in the Bible until I spent those years in jail. I was constantly finding new treasures."

John Bunyan (1628–1688)

God Reveals Himself

THE BIG IDEA

God has always taken the initiative in revealing Himself to humankind.

What You Need to Know

- ▶ God reveals Himself through general revelation and through special revelation.

- ▶ General revelation is available to all persons at all times. It includes the world of nature. "The heavens declare the glory of God, and the sky above proclaims his handiwork" (Psalm 19:1).

- ▶ By observing nature we can detect something of God's existence and discern something of God's divine power and glory.

- ▶ General revelation, however, has limits. It does not provide specific information about our sin problem or the gospel of salvation. That requires special revelation.

His mighty acts in history (Exodus 7–12)

The person of Jesus Christ (Hebrews 1:2-3)

The prophets and apostles, whose writings are in the Bible (Ephesians 2:19-20; 1 Thessalonians 2:13)

Points to Remember

1. God always intended for His revelations to be written down and preserved. For example, Moses, Joshua, and Isaiah wrote in obedience to God's instructions (Exodus 24:4; Joshua 24:26; Isaiah 8:1).

2. Aren't you thankful that God arranged for His revelation to be written down so you and I could read it in the Bible?

A Quote to Ponder

"[The Bible is] God preaching, God talking, God telling, God instructing, God setting before us the right way to think and speak about him."

J.I. Packer

Scripture Is Inspired

THE BIG IDEA

God superintended the human authors of Scripture so that, using their own individual personalities and even their own writing styles, they composed and recorded without error His revelation to humankind.

What You Need to Know

▶ The Bible's authors were from all walks of life—kings, peasants, philosophers, fishermen, physicians, statesmen, scholars, poets, and farmers. They lived in different cultures, had vastly different experiences, and exhibited differing character traits. Yet the Bible has a remarkable continuity that can be observed from Genesis to Revelation.

▶ How did God accomplish this? It's related to a process we call "inspiration." The Greek word translated "inspired" in the Bible literally means "God-breathed."

▶ Because Scripture is breathed out by God—because God is the source of Scripture—it is true and has no errors (see John 17:17; Romans 3:4; 2 Timothy 3:16).

Isaiah wrote with a powerful literary style.

Jeremiah wrote with a mournful tone.

Luke wrote with medical overtones.

John wrote with very simple words.

Points to Remember

1. The Scripture writers were "carried along" by the Holy Spirit in their writings (2 Peter 1:21).

2. This means the authors were not the originators of God's message. God did not permit the will of sinful human beings to misdirect His message.

3. Because Scripture is "breathed out" by God, whatever Scripture affirms or denies, it does so with God's authority.

4. We therefore owe to Scripture the same reverence that we owe to God. To disrespect Scripture is to disrespect God Himself.

A Quote to Ponder

"God moved and the prophet mouthed these truths; God revealed and man recorded His word."
Norman Geisler

4

Scripture Is Inerrant

THE BIG IDEA

Because the Scriptures are inspired by the Holy Spirit, they are wholly inerrant.

What You Need to Know

- As previously noted, the Greek word translated "inspired" literally means "God-breathed."
- Because Scripture is breathed out by God, it is true and has no errors (Proverbs 30:5).
- God is true (Romans 3:4), and God breathed out the Scriptures (2 Timothy 3:16), so the Scriptures are therefore also true (John 17:17).
- Because Scripture is true, you can read your Bible with confidence.

Verses to Contemplate

"Your word is truth" (John 17:17).
"Every word of God proves true" (Proverbs 30:5).

inerrant (John 17:17)

infallible (John 10:35)

imperishable (Matthew 5:17-18)

authoritative (Matthew 4:4,7,10)

historically reliable (Matthew 12:40; 24:37-39)

Points to Remember

Because Scripture is true and inerrant, from Genesis to Revelation, you can trust...

1. its words about your salvation in Jesus Christ (John 20:30-31)

2. its comforting promises (Joshua 21:45)

3. everything it says about your destiny in heaven (Revelation 21:1-5)

A Quote to Ponder

"The Scriptures possess the quality of freedom from error. They are exempt from the liability to make mistakes, and are incapable of error. In all their teachings they are in perfect accord with the truth."

Edward J. Young

13

Eyewitness Testimony

THE BIG IDEA

The Bible's descriptions of events—including Jesus's mighty miracles—are trustworthy because of the abundance of eyewitness testimony.

What You Need to Know

- ▶ Jesus performed miracles in the presence of His disciples to ensure that there was adequate witness to the events that transpired (John 20:30).

- ▶ The noun "witness" is used 14 times in John's Gospel. The verb "testify" is used 33 times. This means Jesus's miracles are thoroughly attested.

- ▶ The witnesses of Jesus's resurrection were also plentiful (see Acts 2:32; 3:15; 5:32; 10:39).

A Key Verse

"We did not follow cleverly devised myths when we made known to you the power and coming of our Lord Jesus Christ, but we were eyewitnesses of his majesty" (2 Peter 1:16).

Points to Remember

1. The eyewitnesses in the New Testament (such as Peter, James, and John) were men of high noble character.

2. These men were schooled from early childhood in the Ten Commandments, including the commandment against bearing false witness (Exodus 20:16). They were thus not prone to misrepresentation.

3. They were willing to give up their lives rather than deny what they knew to be true about Jesus. People don't die in defense of a lie.

4. You can trust all that is written in your Bible!

A Quote to Ponder

"The eyewitness testimony of Jesus's life, teaching, and ministry was carefully recorded and dutifully maintained throughout the centuries."

Chuck Swindoll

The Books in the Bible

THE BIG IDEA

Five tests guided the early church in its recognition of which books belonged in the Bible.

What You Need to Know

- ▶ The book must be written or approved by a prophet or apostle (Deuteronomy 18:18; Galatians 1:11-24; 2 Peter 1:20-21). Luke, for example, was not an apostle, but he was an associate of the apostle Paul. This principle was the most important.

- ▶ The book must be authoritative. It has to ring with the sense of "Thus says the LORD" (Exodus 4:22; 5:1; 7:17).

- ▶ The book must be in agreement with previous revelation (Acts 17:11).

- ▶ The book must exhibit the power of God. God transforms readers' lives through writings that come from Him (2 Timothy 3:16-17; Hebrews 4:12).

- ▶ The book must receive wide acceptance by the people of God (Deuteronomy 31:24-26; 1 Thessalonians 2:13; Colossians 4:16).

Points to Remember

1. Many New Testament books were recognized as Scripture during the time they were written (1 Corinthians 14:37; 1 Thessalonians 2:13; 1 Timothy 5:18; 2 Peter 3:16).

2. God determined and regulated the canon; church leaders met to discover and recognize the canon.

3. This recognition was based on the five canonical tests noted previously, as guided by God.

A Quote to Ponder

"The New Testament books did not become authoritative for the Church because they were formally included in a canonical list; on the contrary, the Church included them in her canon because she already regarded them as divinely inspired."

F.F. Bruce

Manuscript Support

THE BIG IDEA

There is overwhelming manuscript evidence that points to the accurate transmission and reliability of the Bible.

What You Need to Know

- ▶ So far, 5686 partial and complete manuscript copies of the New Testament have been discovered.

- ▶ Many are dated very early, some to within a generation of the original biblical text.

- ▶ If we include the 10,000 Latin Vulgate manuscripts and at least 9300 other early versions (including Ethiopic, Slavic, and Armenian versions), the total approximates 25,000 manuscripts that cite portions of the New Testament.

- ▶ The early church fathers and several thousand lectionaries (church-service books from the early centuries of Christianity) include more than 36,000 quotations of the New Testament. Even if we didn't have a single New Testament manuscript, we could reconstruct all but 11 verses of the New Testament from these writings alone.

Points to Remember

1. We have very few copies of other ancient literary works (such as the writings of Plato and Josephus), but nobody doubts their accurate transmission.

2. How much more should we be confident of the accurate transmission of the Bible, which has staggering manuscript support.

3. We need not accept the Bible only by faith. It has solid manuscript support that proves its accurate transmission.

A Quote to Ponder

"The interval then between the dates of the original composition and the earliest extant evidence becomes so small as to be in fact negligible."

Sir Frederic Kenyon

Manuscript Differences

THE BIG IDEA

The variations between the New Testament manuscript copies are minor. None are significant.

What You Need to Know

- ▶ Scholars have discovered more than 200,000 minor alterations in the New Testament manuscript copies.

- ▶ The sheer volume of manuscripts (more than 25,000) greatly narrows the margin of doubt regarding what the original biblical documents said.

- ▶ The great majority of variants are minor, such as misspellings or differences in word order.

FAST FACTS
How Errors Might Have Occurred

A copyist reading an earlier text might have misread it.

A copyist listening to manuscript dictation might have inserted a word that sounded the same.

In early biblical manuscripts, letters were not separated into words with spaces. ("Heisnowhere" could mean "he is now here" or "he is nowhere.")

Points to Remember

1. Bible scholars use well-defined principles to confirm the original text. For example, readings are preferred if they are shorter (scribes tended to add clarifying words), have the widest geographical support, conform to the style of the author, and best explain the variants.

2. Scholars who respect and are committed to the Word of God have used these methods to ascertain more than 99 percent of the original text to a virtual certainty.

3. You can trust your Bible!

A Quote to Ponder

"If the number of [manuscripts] increases the number of scribal errors, it increases proportionately the means of correcting such errors, so that the margin of doubt left in the process of recovering the exact original wording is not so large as might be feared; it is in truth remarkably small."

F.F. Bruce

The Dead Sea Scrolls

THE BIG IDEA

The Dead Sea Scrolls provide convincing proof for the accuracy of the transmission of biblical manuscripts.

What You Need to Know

▶ Thousands of fragments belonging to more than 800 manuscripts have been discovered in 11 different caves at Qumran, near the shores of the Dead Sea.

▶ Forty percent are Old Testament manuscripts. These manuscripts (dated at 150 BC) are about a thousand years earlier than our previous Old Testament manuscripts (dated at AD 980).

▶ The scrolls are essentially the same as our other manuscripts with few changes.

▶ The scrolls verify that biblical manuscripts were copied accurately.

The Isaiah Scrolls

Two copies of Isaiah were found. The majority of verses are identical to our Hebrew text. The variations are minor—typically slips of the pen and variations in spelling.

Points to Remember

1. The Dead Sea Scrolls prove that the copyists of biblical manuscripts went to incredible lengths to ensure that errors did not creep into the biblical text. They carefully counted every line, word, syllable, and letter to ensure accuracy.

2. We can have a high level of confidence that the Scriptures have been faithfully transmitted to us.

3. You can trust your Bible!

A Quote to Ponder

"Even though the two copies of Isaiah discovered in Qumran Cave 1 near the Dead Sea in 1947 were a thousand years earlier than the oldest dated manuscript previously known (AD 980), they proved to be word-for-word identical with our standard Hebrew Bible in more than 95 percent of the text."

Gleason Archer

God's Preservational Providence

THE BIG IDEA

There is evidence that God preserved His Word in the transmission of the biblical manuscripts from one generation to the next.

What You Need to Know

▶ Jesus implicitly assumed the preservation of His Word. "This gospel of the kingdom will be proclaimed throughout the whole world...and then the end will come" (Matthew 24:14; see 28:19-20).

▶ For the gospel to be preached in all the world until "the end," the Word of God must be preserved from age to age.

Jesus's Treatment of the Old Testament

Jesus did not possess the original manuscripts of the Old Testament writers. He had only copies, yet He had full confidence that the Old Testament Scriptures He used had been faithfully preserved through the centuries (see, for example, Matthew 4:4,7,10; 5:17-19).

"Moses wrote down all the words of the LORD" (Exodus 24:4).

"Joshua wrote these words in the Book of the Law of God" (Joshua 24:26).

"Samuel...wrote them in a book" (1 Samuel 10:25).

Isaiah wrote on a large tablet (Isaiah 8:1).

Paul wrote commands of the Lord (1 Corinthians 14:37).

Points to Remember

1. Jesus and His apostles were confident that God providentially preserved the Word of God in their copies of the Old Testament.
2. Likewise, we today can trust that both the Old and New Testaments are accurately preserved in our manuscript copies.

A Quote to Ponder

"Because Christ raised no doubts about the adequacy of the Scripture as His contemporaries knew them, we can safely assume that the first-century text of the Old Testament was a wholly adequate representation of the divine word originally given."

Greg Bahnsen

Archaeological Support

THE BIG IDEA

Substantial archaeological evidence verifies the Old and New Testaments.

What You Need to Know

"Archaeology" comes from two Greek words—*archaios*, meaning "ancient things," and *logos*, meaning "study of." Archaeology is the study of ancient things. It is beneficial to Bible study because it...

- ▶ provides the historical context of the Bible
- ▶ provides helpful background information on people, places, and events in the Bible
- ▶ helps illuminate Scripture
- ▶ verifies the reliability of the Bible

For Example...

Archaeology provides information on the flood of Noah's day, the Hebrew slaves making bricks in Egypt, Egypt's many false gods, the lower city wall in Jericho, and David's and Solomon's empires.

Points to Remember

1. More than 25,000 archaeological discoveries over a wide geographical area support the truth of the Bible.
2. Not a single archaeological discovery has ever controverted what we find in the Bible.
3. The more we dig up in biblical lands, the more we find support for people, places, and events recorded in the Bible.
4. We can confidently say that archaeology is a friend of the Bible.

A Quote to Ponder

"Discovery after discovery has established the accuracy of innumerable details, and has brought increased recognition of the value of the Bible as a source of history."

William F. Albright

Extrabiblical Non-Christian Support

THE BIG IDEA

There are a number of extrabiblical (outside of the Bible) non-Christian sources that mention various aspects of Jesus's life, thus lending support to the Bible.

What You Need to Know

▶ Josephus (AD 37–100) was a Jewish historian. He corroborates that Jesus was the leader of Christians, that He did wonderful works, and that He was crucified for the Christian cause.

▶ Pliny (AD 62–113), a Roman governor, verifies that Christians worshipped Jesus as God.

▶ Tacitus (AD 56-117), a Roman historian, refers to people's belief in Jesus's crucifixion and resurrection.

▶ The Talmud, rabbinic writings from around AD 200, mentions the belief in Jesus's virgin birth, miracles, and crucifixion.

FAST FACTS
Extrabiblical Evidence Says Jesus...

was a wonder worker	was worshipped as God
lived a virtuous life	was crucified under Pilate
had a brother named James	was believed to be resurrected
was acclaimed as Messiah	

Points to Remember

1. The multiple extrabiblical references to Jesus and the early Christians prove that Christianity is not a myth or a legend, but rather is founded in history.
2. Extrabiblical sources validate key details of what is recorded in the New Testament.
3. This includes numerous details about the life and ministry of Christ.
4. You can trust your Bible!

A Quote to Ponder

"[Christians] were in the habit of meeting on a certain fixed day before it was light, when they sang in alternate verses a hymn to Christ, as to a god."

Pliny the Younger (about AD 112)

13

Extrabiblical Christian Support

THE BIG IDEA

A number of extrabiblical Christian sources mention various aspects of Jesus's life, thus lending support to the Bible, especially the four Gospels.

What You Need to Know

▶ Clement, an elder in Rome in AD 95, referred to the Gospels as Scripture and said they contain the actual words of Jesus.

▶ Papias, bishop of Hierapolis in AD 130, affirmed the same things.

▶ Justin Martyr, an apologist in AD 140, also said the four Gospels were Scripture. He discussed the crucifixion and resurrection: "After He [Jesus] was crucified, even all His acquaintances forsook Him, having denied Him." Afterward, "when He had risen from the dead and appeared to them," they went out and "taught these things, and were called apostles." Justin died as a martyr instead of betraying the truth about Jesus Christ and Christianity.

FAST FACTS
The Didache

The Didache was a manual of Christianity written in the late first century.

It cites portions of the three synoptic Gospels and refers to them as the actual words of Jesus.

This manual quotes extensively from Matthew's Gospel.

Points to Remember

1. Many early Christian sources dating between AD 95 and 150 refer to Matthew, Mark, Luke, and John as containing the actual words of Christ.

2. History is therefore on the side of the New Testament Gospels and argues against the skeptical claim that they contain myths.

3. Extrabiblical Christian and non-Christian sources that refer to Jesus boost confidence in the truth of the biblical account.

A Quote to Ponder

"In many places these [early extrabiblical Christian] writings attest to the basic facts about Jesus, particularly His teachings, His crucifixion, His resurrection, and His divine nature."

Lee Strobel

Christ's View of Scripture

THE BIG IDEA

Jesus confirmed that the Scriptures are the Word of God; that they are inerrant, infallible, and eternal; and that they carry the authority of God.

What You Need to Know

Jesus affirmed that Scripture is...

▶ inspired by the Holy Spirit (Matthew 22:43), inerrant (John 17:17), and infallible (John 10:35)

▶ reliable (Matthew 26:54), historically accurate (Matthew 12:40), and consistent (Luke 24:27,44)

▶ authoritative (Matthew 4:4,7,10), eternal (Matthew 5:18), and fully sufficient (Luke 16:31)

Jesus's Promises About the Writing of the New Testament

Jesus promised that the Holy Spirit would guide the disciples (John 14:25-26) into all the truth (John 16:13). These promises were fulfilled (see 2 Timothy 3:16; 1 Thessalonians 2:13).

The Written Word	The Incarnate Word
was inspired by the Holy Spirit	was conceived by the Holy Spirit
uses common language	appeared as a common man
is perfectly inerrant	is perfectly sinless

Points to Remember

Jesus confirmed the historicity of a number of disputed Old Testament people and events, including...

1. the creation (Luke 11:50)
2. Adam and Eve (Matthew 19:4-5)
3. Noah and the flood (Matthew 24:37-39)
4. Sodom and Gomorrah (Luke 10:12)
5. Jonah and the great fish (Matthew 12:39-41)

A Quote to Ponder

"Jesus frequently used the Scripture as the proof text from which He both substantiated His view, as well as refuted the improper views held by others. He relied on Scripture for what it was—the very Word of God."

Gary Habermas

The Apostles' View of Scripture

THE BIG IDEA

The apostles became the agents of the complete and final revelation of Jesus Christ. They recognized that their writings were divinely inspired.

What You Need to Know

▶ The apostles recognized that God was providing revelation through them (1 Corinthians 2:13; 1 Thessalonians 2:13; 1 John 1:1-3).

▶ The apostles were guided into all truth by the Spirit of truth as they wrote (John 14:26; 16:13).

▶ They recognized their divine authority (Acts 20:35; 1 Corinthians 7:10; 11:23-24).

▶ They were authenticated by miraculous signs (Acts 3:3-10; 5:15-16; 9:36-42; 20:7-12).

No Apostles Today

Apostles were eyewitnesses to the resurrection of Christ (see 1 Corinthians 9:1). No one living today witnessed the resurrection of Christ, so there can be no apostles and no continuing biblical revelation today.

Points to Remember

1. The early church built its doctrines and practices on "the foundation of the apostles and prophets" (Ephesians 2:20).
2. The early believers "devoted themselves to the apostles' teaching" (Acts 2:42).
3. Throughout Acts the pronouncements of the apostles were final (Acts 15).
4. You and I are to build our doctrine and practices on Scripture and devote ourselves to its teachings. Scriptural pronouncements are final.

A Quote to Ponder

"Since the apostles' teaching about Christ is itself revealed truth in God-taught words (1 Cor. 2:12-13), the church rightly regards authentic apostolic writings as completing the Scriptures."

J.I. Packer

Prophecy as a Proof

THE BIG IDEA

Fulfilled prophecy constitutes a convincing proof of the inspiration and inerrancy of Scripture.

What You Need to Know

▶ From Genesis to Malachi, the Old Testament anticipates the coming Messiah.

▶ More than 100 predictions of Jesus's birth, ministry, death, resurrection, and glory were fulfilled in the New Testament.

▶ These fulfilled prophecies constitute a powerful apologetic for the inspiration of Scripture.

Two Key Verses

"I am God, and there is no other; I am God, and there is none like me, declaring the end from the beginning and from ancient times things not yet done, saying, 'My counsel shall stand, and I will accomplish all my purpose'" (Isaiah 46:9-10).

"All this has taken place that the Scriptures of the prophets might be fulfilled" (Matthew 26:56).

FAST FACTS
A Sampling of Prophecies About Christ

He was born of a virgin (Isaiah 7:14) in Bethlehem (Micah 5:2).

He performed miracles (Isaiah 35:5-6).

He suffered thirst (Psalm 69:21) and was crucified (Isaiah 53:12).

He was resurrected (Psalm 16:10).

Points to Remember

1. These prophecies were written many hundreds of years before they were fulfilled. They depended on factors outside human control for their fulfillment.
2. All of these prophecies were precisely fulfilled.
3. Clearly the Scriptures are divine in origin and not man-made. Predictive prophecy is a powerful proof that the Bible is God's Word (Isaiah 46:10).

A Quote to Ponder

"Hundreds of prophecies have come to pass exactly as the Bible has said, which is absolute proof that the Bible is the inspired Word of the Sovereign Lord."

Mark Hitchcock

Assessing the Miracle Accounts

THE BIG IDEA

The miracle accounts in the Bible are trustworthy and cannot be dismissed as myths.

What You Need to Know

▶ Critics dismiss miracles because they appear to violate the laws of nature.

▶ When God miraculously intervenes in His creation, however, the laws of nature are not violated. They are simply superseded by a higher law—God's will.

▶ The forces of nature are not suspended, but are only counteracted at a particular point by a force superior to the powers of nature.

God's Purpose for Miracles

Miracles accredit God's messengers (Hebrews 2:3-4), glorify God the Father and God the Son (John 2:11), promote faith among God's people (Exodus 14:31; John 20:30-31), and demonstrate God's sovereignty (Exodus 7:5; Deuteronomy 29:5-6).

There were countless eyewitnesses (1 Corinthians 15:6).

The Bible writers told the truth (Exodus 20:16).

They died in defense of the truth (John 21:18-19).

Points to Remember

1. Liberal Bible critics are biased against all things supernatural. They reject the possibility that anything exists beyond the natural world.

2. The biblical worldview is comprehensive, embracing both the natural world and the supernatural world.

3. A belief in miracles does not undermine the Bible, but rather establishes the truth of the Bible. That is, miracles in Bible times verified the truth spoken by the prophets and apostles.

4. You can trust your Bible!

A Quote to Ponder

"If there is a God who can act, then there can be acts of God. The only way to show that miracles are impossible is to disprove the existence of God."

Norman Geisler

18

Theories of Bible Translation

THE BIG IDEA

Some Bible translations are designed to be as literal as possible. Others are designed to be as readable as possible. Both seek to glorify God.

What You Need to Know

- The *formal equivalence* approach advocates a literal rendering that is form-for-form or word-for-word. This approach preserves the original beauty of Scripture, retains necessary theological terminology, and avoids too much interpretive commentary.

- The *dynamic equivalence* approach advocates a more readable translation. It does not provide an exact rendering of the text, but rather focuses on communicating the meaning of the text. It is a thought-for-thought, meaning-driven translation that seeks to produce the same dynamic impact on modern readers that the original had upon its audience.

Points to Remember

1. Formal equivalence Bibles are excellent study Bibles because they are quite literal.
2. Dynamic equivalence Bibles make reading the Bible easier so you can understand its meaning.
3. There is benefit in using both a formal equivalence Bible and a dynamic equivalence Bible.

A Quote to Ponder

"If the apostles wrote in easy-to-understand terms, then translations of the Bible should reflect this. We ought not to translate with big 50-cent religious-sounding words if the original was not written that way."

Daniel Wallace

19

The Interpretation of Scripture

THE BIG IDEA

We can use sound interpretive principles to clearly understand the meaning of each Bible verse.

What You Need to Know

▶ Seek the author's intended meaning instead of superimposing a meaning onto the text.

▶ Pay close attention to the context. Each verse is related to the verses around it.

▶ Interpret the difficult verses in light of the clear verses.

▶ Interpret the Old Testament according to the greater light of the New Testament.

▶ Consult history and culture to help you understand Bible times better.

▶ Make a correct genre judgment. Different genres have different characteristics.

A Key Verse

"Do your best to present yourself to God as one approved, a worker who has no need to be ashamed, rightly handling the word of truth" (2 Timothy 2:15.)

Points to Remember

1. We must all depend on the Holy Spirit for illumination of God's Word.
2. The Holy Spirit inspired Scripture (2 Timothy 3:16) and is therefore its best interpreter (John 16:13; 1 Corinthians 2:12).
3. Always pray for the Spirit's help (Psalm 119:18).

A Quote to Ponder

"When the plain sense of Scripture makes common sense, seek no other sense; therefore, take every word at its primary, ordinary, usual, literal meaning unless the facts of the immediate context...indicate clearly otherwise."

David Cooper

The Bible Is a "Jesus Book"

THE BIG IDEA

From Genesis to Revelation, the Bible is a "Jesus book."

What You Need to Know

Jesus is the heart of the Bible (Matthew 5:17; John 5:39-40). He is therefore at the heart of every Christian doctrine. For example...

- ▶ Jesus is the ultimate revelation of God (Hebrews 1:2-3,8).

- ▶ Jesus is the Creator of the universe (Colossians 1:16).

- ▶ Salvation is found in Jesus (John 3:16).

- ▶ Jesus is the Head of the church (Colossians 1:18).

Verses to Contemplate

Jesus affirmed that the Scriptures were written about Him (Luke 24:27,44; John 5:39; Hebrews 10:7).

Points to Remember

1. A relationship with Jesus is the heart of Christianity. Without Jesus there would be no Christianity.

2. To know Jesus is to know God. To see Jesus is to see God. To believe in Jesus is to believe in God. To receive Jesus is to receive God. To honor Jesus is to honor God. To worship Jesus is to worship God.

3. Is your Christianity as Jesus-centered as the Bible indicates it should be?

A Quote to Ponder

*"Christianity is not devotion to work, or to a cause,
or a doctrine, but devotion to a person,
the Lord Jesus Christ."*

Oswald Chambers

21

God's Promises in Scripture

THE BIG IDEA

Scripture is brimming with God's promises relating to many different areas of our spiritual lives.

What You Need to Know

▶ God is a promise keeper (Numbers 23:19).

▶ His promises never fail; He always fulfills them (Joshua 23:14; 1 Kings 8:56).

Two Key Verses

"God is not man, that he should lie, or a son of man, that he should change his mind. Has he said, and will he not do it? Or has he spoken, and will he not fulfill it?" (Numbers 23:19).

"Not one word has failed of all the good things that the LORD your God promised concerning you. All have come to pass for you; not one of them has failed" (Joshua 23:14).

Some are conditional (James 1:25).

Others are unconditional (Galatians 4:6-7).

Don't claim as a promise of God something a mere human said (Job 4:8; 8:6).

Promises made to specific individuals are not intended for all believers (Isaiah 38:5).

Promises to Old Testament Israelites may not be promises to us today (Deuteronomy 28:15-68).

Points to Remember

1. "Faith is the assurance of things hoped for, the conviction of things not seen" (Hebrews 11:1).
2. God Himself is with us, awaiting our response to His presence and to His many promises.
3. This spiritual world will come alive to us the moment we begin to reckon upon its reality and believe God's promises (see 2 Kings 6:8-23).

A Quote to Ponder

"What greater rebellion, impiety, or insult to God can there be than not to believe His promises?"

Martin Luther

22

The Application of Scripture

THE BIG IDEA

It is not enough to simply understand Scripture. We must apply it to our lives.

What You Need to Know

▶ Bible application involves bringing our lives into conformity with the truths of Scripture.

▶ We must be doers of the Word, not just hearers (James 1:22).

▶ We should maintain a predetermined attitude of absolute obedience to what we learn in Scripture (1 Samuel 15:22; Psalm 119:2).

▶ The goal is to be transformed (Romans 12:2).

▶ Walking in dependence on the Holy Spirit produces the fruit of transformation (Galatians 5:16-26).

A Key Verse

"All Scripture is breathed out by God and profitable for teaching, for reproof, for correction, and for training in righteousness, that the man of God may be complete, equipped for every good work" (2 Timothy 3:16-17).

Points to Remember

1. Scripture exhorts us, "Examine yourselves, to see whether you are in the faith" (2 Corinthians 13:5). Ask...

   - Am I walking the walk and not just talking the talk? Am I just playing a game, or is my spirituality genuine?
   - If I were accused of being a Christian, would there be enough evidence to convict me?
   - Am I a secret-agent Christian who has never blown his cover?
   - Is my life changing as I read Scripture and walk with Christ?

2. Self-examination is not always comfortable. But it is necessary because it can motivate us to make midcourse changes in the direction of our lives. It's never too late to submit to Scripture.

3. Make a resolution to purposefully submit to being transformed by God's Word.

A Quote to Ponder

"Heart appropriation, not merely head apprehension, is the true goal of Bible study."
Roy Zuck

23

Assessing Alleged Contradictions

THE BIG IDEA

The Gospels may have some *apparent* contradictions, but they have no *genuine* contradictions.

What You Need to Know

- ▶ There are differences among the four Gospels but not genuine contradictions.

- ▶ If all four Gospels were virtually the same, critics would accuse the writers of collusion.

- ▶ Let's not confuse human fallible interpretations with God's infallible biblical revelation.

- ▶ Context often clears up apparent contradictions.

- ▶ Remember that a partial account is not a false account.

- ▶ Be sure to interpret the difficult verses in light of the clearer verses.

- ▶ Do not presume that the Bible approves of all that it records (such as the words of Satan).

► Citations of Old Testament verses in the New Testament need not be exact.

Points to Remember

Apparent Bible contradictions tend to be cleared up as we...

1. continue studying the Bible
2. learn more about biblical history
3. broaden our understanding of biblical culture and customs
4. glean more insights from the original languages of the Bible (Hebrew and Greek)

A Quote to Ponder

"If we are perplexed by any apparent contradiction in Scripture, it is not allowable to say, the author of this book is mistaken; but either the manuscript is faulty, or the translation is wrong, or you have not understood."

Augustine

24

Assessing Objections to the Bible

THE BIG IDEA

As a case study, liberal critics say evolution contradicts the biblical creation account and thereby undermines the Bible.

What You Need to Know

- ▶ Most scientists and philosophers agree that the universe had a beginning. This implies a Beginner—a Creator.

- ▶ Observing the universe provides evidence of an intelligent Designer, who is God.

- ▶ The fossil records argue against evolution (there are no transitional fossils).

- ▶ Almost all mutations are harmful, but evolution assumes countless positive mutations.

- ▶ The second law of thermodynamics proves our universe is running down, not evolving upward.

- ▶ DNA is packed with complex information. Where did it come from? It can only be from God.

Two Key Verses

"Every house is built by someone, but the builder of all things is God" (Hebrews 3:4).

"The heavens declare the glory of God, and the sky above proclaims his handiwork" (Psalm 19:1).

Points to Remember

1. An unbiased look at the evidence provides convincing proof that creationism is true.

2. We can trust not only the creation account in Scripture but also everything else found within its pages.

3. Don't let your faith be injured by secularist claims that purport to disprove the Bible.

4. "See to it that no one takes you captive by philosophy and empty deceit, according to human tradition" (Colossians 2:8).

A Quote to Ponder

"It is absurd for the evolutionists to complain that it's unthinkable for an admittedly unthinkable God to make everything out of nothing and then pretend it is more thinkable that nothing should turn itself into anything."

G.K. Chesterton

Assessing the Apocrypha

THE BIG IDEA

The Apocrypha is a collection of books of doubtful authenticity that were written between Old and New Testament times. Protestant Christians reject them from the biblical canon.

The Catholic–Protestant Debate

Roman Catholics believe the Apocrypha belongs in the Bible because it was in the Septuagint (an early Greek translation of the Old Testament) and because some church fathers accepted it. Protestants disagree because...

▶ Jesus and the disciples ignored it, no New Testament writer quoted it, and an early Jewish council and some church fathers rejected it.

▶ It contains historical errors and unbiblical doctrines.

▶ It contains no claim of divine inspiration and no predictive prophecy, and it was not confirmed by divine miracles.

A historical error: Tobit 1:15 names Sennacherib as the son of Shalmaneser. He was actually the son of Sargon II.

A doctrinal error: Second Maccabees 12:42-45 refers to the doctrine of the Mass (but contrast Hebrews 7:27).

Points to Remember

1. There were five specific tests for canonicity: Books had to be written or backed by a prophet or apostle, be authoritative, agree with previous divine revelation, exhibit the power of God, and be accepted by the people of God.

2. The Apocrypha fails these tests. The books in the Protestant Bible pass.

3. It is therefore wisest to choose a Bible that does not contain the Apocrypha.

A Quote to Ponder

"Philo makes no quotations from the Apocrypha; and he gives not the slightest ground for the supposition that the Jews of Alexandria, in his time, were disposed to accept any of the books of the Apocrypha in their Canon of Holy Scripture."

H.E. Ryle

26

Assessing the Gnostic Gospels

THE BIG IDEA

The gnostic gospels are forgeries that date far after New Testament times.

What You Need to Know

- ▶ Gnostics taught that spirit is good and matter is evil. Therefore they believed Jesus did not have a physical body.

- ▶ Early church apologists, such as Irenaeus (AD 130–200) and Origen (AD 185–253), said these false gospels were full of deception and heresy.

- ▶ The earliest gnostic gospels may date as early as AD 150, but most date in the third and fourth centuries—far too late to be reliable.

- ▶ The New Testament includes eyewitness accounts, but these late gospels do not.

- ▶ These gospels are forgeries (for example, the gospel of Thomas was not written by the biblical Thomas).

Points to Remember

1. The New Testament Gospels are dated very early, close in time to the events on which they report. Early Gospels are reliable Gospels.

2. The New Testament Gospels have strong manuscript support and strong archaeological support, and they are verified by extrabiblical secular writers (such as Tacitus and Pliny the Younger).

3. The gnostic gospels have an uphill battle against the authentic Gospels.

4. You can trust your Bible!

A Quote to Ponder

"...an unspeakable number of apocryphal and spurious writings, which they themselves [heretics] had forged, to bewilder the minds of the foolish."
Irenaeus (AD 130–200)

27

Assessing Other "Holy Books"

THE BIG IDEA

Other so-called holy books, such as the Muslim Quran and the Hindu Vedas, do not contain the Word of God, as the Bible does.

What You Need to Know

▶ The Bible is not one among many holy books.

▶ If the Bible contains the Word of God, the others cannot contain the Word of God because they contradict the Bible at countless points.

▶ Many ideas in other holy books are diametrically opposed to those found in the Bible.

Example: The Doctrine of God

The Bible teaches God is a Trinity. But the Quran teaches that God cannot have a son, Confucius's writings teach that there are many gods, and Buddha's writings teach that God is irrelevant. Contradictory views cannot all be right, so the Bible alone—the true Word of God— is right, as this entire book demonstrates.

Unity. The 66 books all center on Jesus.

Preservation. The Bible has unmatched manuscript support.

Proclamations. The Bible contains dead-accurate predictive prophecies.

Points to Remember

1. Jesus was unbendingly exclusive in His truth claims, indicating that His words took precedence over all others.

2. Jesus said He is man's only means of coming into a relationship with God: "I am the way, and the truth, and the life. No one comes to the Father except through me" (John 14:6).

3. There is one true holy book—the Bible. There is one true Savior—Jesus Christ.

A Quote to Ponder

"Webster must have had this 'Book of books' [the Bible] in mind when he wrote the definition for 'unique': '1. one and only; single; sole. 2. different from all others; having no like or equal.'"

Josh McDowell

Assessing Tradition

THE BIG IDEA

Tradition (such as a church confession) may be of historic value, but it is not inspired, and it is not on the level of Scripture.

What You Need to Know

Some Christians who emphasize tradition reject the idea of *sola Scriptura* ("Scripture alone"). They believe both Scripture and tradition constitute the Word of God and that the Bible cannot be correctly interpreted without tradition. However...

▶ Scripture alone speaks with God's voice and is authoritative in matters of faith and practice.

▶ Tradition is to be respected but not exalted to the level of Scripture, for only Scripture is inspired by the Holy Spirit (2 Timothy 3:16).

▶ The Lord Jesus always used Scripture as His final court of appeal (Matthew 4:4-10).

▶ The apostle Paul affirmed the full adequacy of Scripture alone (2 Timothy 3:16-17).

A Warning from Jesus

Jesus criticized some Jewish leaders by saying, "You leave the commandment of God and hold to the tradition of men...thus making void the word of God by your tradition that you have handed down" (Mark 7:8,13).

Points to Remember

1. Tradition is not necessary to understand Scripture.
2. Tradition itself is often hard to understand and needs to be deciphered.
3. The Bible is sufficiently clear in its teachings. The main things are the plain things and the plain things are the main things.
4. The Holy Spirit is our teacher. He illumines Scripture and guides us so we can understand it (1 Corinthians 2:12-13).

A Quote to Ponder

"The Reformation principle of sola Scriptura *has to do with the sufficiency of Scripture as our supreme authority in all spiritual matters. Sola Scriptura simply means that all truth necessary for our salvation and spiritual life is taught either explicitly or implicitly in Scripture."*

R.C. Sproul

The Full Sufficiency of Scripture

THE BIG IDEA

The Word of God is sufficient to teach us all we need to know on spiritual matters.

What You Need to Know

The Word of God is fully sufficient to...

- ▶ teach us about sin and our need for salvation through Christ (2 Timothy 3:15)

- ▶ reprove us, correct us, and train us on spiritual and moral matters (2 Timothy 3:16-17)

- ▶ provide spiritual direction in life (Psalm 119:105)

- ▶ revive and restore our souls (Psalm 19:7)

- ▶ provide comfort in tough times (Psalm 23)

- ▶ bring us spiritual joy (Psalm 19:8)

A Quote to Ponder

"God's Word is sufficient to meet every need of the human soul...Scripture is comprehensive, containing everything necessary for one's spiritual life...Scripture contains divine principles that are the best guide for character and conduct."

John MacArthur

Bibliography

Bruce, F.F. *The New Testament Documents: Are They Reliable?* Grand Rapids, MI: Eerdmans, 1978.

Geisler, Norman, and William Nix. *From God to Us: How We Got Our Bible.* Chicago, IL: Moody, 2012.

Geisler, Norman, and William Nix. *A General Introduction to the Bible.* Chicago, IL: Moody, 1978.

Hannah, John D., ed. *Inerrancy and the Church.* Chicago, IL: Moody, 1984.

Lutzer, Erwin W. *Seven Reasons Why You Can Trust the Bible.* Chicago, IL: Moody, 2008.

McDowell, Josh. *The New Evidence That Demands a Verdict.* Nashville: Thomas Nelson, 1999.

Packer, J.I. *Honoring the Written Word of God.* Vancouver: Regent College Publishing, 2002.

Rhodes, Ron. *The Big Book of Bible Answers.* Eugene, OR: Harvest House, 2013.

Rhodes, Ron. *The Complete Guide to Bible Translations.* Eugene, OR: Harvest House, 2009.

Sproul, R.C. *Can I Trust the Bible?* Sanford, FL: Reformation Trust Publishing, 2009.

Strobel, Lee. *The Case for Faith.* Grand Rapids, MI: Zondervan, 2000.

Warfield, Benjamin B. *The Inspiration and Authority of the Bible.* Phillipsburg, NJ: P&R, 1948.

To learn more about Harvest House books and
to read sample chapters, log on to our website:

www.harvesthousepublishers.com

HARVEST HOUSE PUBLISHERS
EUGENE, OREGON